# The Ultimate

# VACATION RENTAL

# Success Guide

## For New and Experienced Owners

# STEVE SCHWAB

ISBN: 978-1530355631

First Printing: April, 2016

Published by 102nd Place LLC
Scottsdale, AZ 85266

# Table of Contents

# INTRODUCTION

Welcome to the family. We're excited that you've joined us and look forward to working in partnership with you to maximize the enjoyment and income from your vacation rental property.

When I say I'm welcoming you into our family, that's exactly what I mean. We treat and manage your property as if it were our own. After all, we're owners ourselves and can easily relate to your questions and concerns. We want to make sure that your vacation rental experience is positive so you can enjoy all the benefits that come with ownership without having to worry about all the little day-to-day details.

Our number one priority is to meet the needs of our homeowners, to exceed every expectation. We are your advocates; acting as your proxy in dealings with guests and service providers. That is the main reason I've assembled this little book.

Most likely your agent explained a lot of the information contained in these pages when reviewing your decision to join us. Some of it you might even find in the welcome packet you received. But what I've discovered is that the information that gets disseminated in these ways often is lost once the ink is dry and the packet is put away.

This book is designed to be a handy reference. First it covers the highlights of what you should expect from us as your property management company. Then we'll talk about the responsibilities that you have as an owner. We'll hit the area of wear and tear versus damages in great detail as I've found this is often the most difficult concept for vacation rental owners to wrap their heads around. I'll end with a section on how to set your renters' expectations and more importantly, how to set the expectations of your family and friends!

I've been in the vacation rental business for over 17 years: as a renter, a rental owner, and now as a successful owner of a property management firm. I've seen some horror stories, but I have had many more magical moments created for families who have rented my properties.

Let's make some magic!

To our success,

*Steve Schwab*

# PROPERTY MANAGEMENT RESPONSIBILITIES

The decision to become a vacation rental owner is rarely made lightly. You've likely invested a significant amount of time and money to ensure that the property you've selected meets your personal vacation dreams, as well as having the potential to meet your future financial goals. It isn't easy to turn management of such a special asset over to a company you've just met.

That is why we are so honored to have been selected to be the servicer for your property. There is a saying that people do business with people they know, like and trust. We've gotten to know you a little, we like you a lot, and now we want to make sure that we continue to build the mutual trust in our ongoing relationship. Trust means building rapport, listening, anticipating your needs, proactively volunteering information, avoiding problems in advance, and efficient, effective service recovery if problems occur.

In this section I will recap our primary responsibilities. And I'm going to start with a topic that is the number one priority for me and my company: ethics.

## Ethics

Merriam-Webster Dictionary defines ethics as: *rules of behavior based on ideas of what is morally good or bad.*

You'll notice that the definition says "morally" not "legally." There's a big difference here – at least to my way of thinking. For example: if we represent a property that is located next to a railroad track we would disclose that to a prospective guest. Legally we are not required to do so, but morally it's the right thing to do.

There are many property managers out there who readily take advantage of both owners and renters. They are the ones who give the industry a bad name. I want to change that.

We are committed to treating you, and your renters, honestly and fairly. It starts with the marketing of your property and goes all the way to payment of revenues. We communicate frequently so that you always know what is happening with your home. And we share with you the survey results from renters regardless if they are good or bad.

Communication is key – it's what builds relationships and trust. We encourage the dialogue to flow both ways. Call us any time you have a question or concern. We're here to help.

## Marketing

Word of mouth is great for getting rental referrals but nothing beats good old-fashioned marketing for reaching a larger pool of candidates in a shorter period of time.

Over our 20 plus years in the business we've written thousands of ads. We know exactly what to say and where to say it to generate a high number of *qualified* applicants for your property. Our brokers and agents are sales people who have the talent to close, whether discussing with a prospect by phone or taking them on a showing.

Rest assured we have you covered. Marketing locally, nationally and internationally, we employ a multi-level strategy to maximize occupancy. We market your property through our own website which receives 7.5 million hits per month. In addition we advertise in online marketplaces such as HomeAway, VRBO, Flipkey, AirBnB, and others. Our calendars synchronize with these third parties' calendars for maximum exposure and lead management.

Our software is also designed to integrate with GDS (Global Distribution Systems) and wholesalers such as Booking.com, Expedia.com and Hotels.com. I personally visit Austin, Texas each year to meet with the leaders of VRBO and HomeAway.com to insure we receive maximum exposure and discounts for our property owners and guests. This would be impossible for the average vacation rental owner to do on their own.

INSTEAD OF 5 MILLION VISITORS PER MONTH, WITH ONLY HOMEAWAY, VRBO, BOOKING.COM, EXPEDIA, AND AIRBNB YOU ARE GETTING MUCH MORE:

OUR OTHER SITES: 8 MILLION PER MONTH COMBINED
ADDED TOGETHER YOU WILL HAVE ABOUT 262.5 MILLION VISITORS PER MONTH.

We only use professional photos when marketing your home. A professional photographer knows exactly what angles, lighting, and features to use to capture your vacation rental at its best. Great looking photos set your home apart from all the others.

## Setting Rates (Seasonal Rentals have a Season)

Setting the appropriate rental rate to insure that your property has maximum occupancy is more an art than a science. It requires a thorough knowledge of the area, data on comparables and competition, and access to rental rate tools. Remember, you aren't just competing against other vacation rental owners. You're also being stacked up against resorts and hotels.

One of the key components of rate is seasonality. Unless your rental is in a year-round destination location or a place like San Diego or the Florida Keys, chances are it has a season. There is a particular time of the year that vacationers will flock to your destination and other times that they will not.

It is important to understand that based on this seasonality, your income from the property will fluctuate as well. For example: if your property is a winter escape destination then your rates will be set higher in the months of December through March when demand is high. You'll see increased income in those months. But once the "season" has passed, in order to maintain occupancy, your rates may need to be adjusted and your income in those months may fall. That's the way the industry works. It's nothing to be concerned about, just something to know and plan for.

Speaking of planning, if the primary goal for owning your vacation rental is income generation, try to book your personal enjoyment of the property to avoid "high" season. If you don't, you may be missing out on what could be some significant income.

## Pricing Strategy

What we like to do is create a pricing strategy that gets you booked first when it is slow in order to keep occupancy going. The strategy is also designed to let the low-ballers get off the market first so you can rent for the highest rate for your property.

We use all of our knowledge of comps in the area, single family homes, condos, townhouses, resorts, etc. to determine a monthly base rate for both in and out of season. Then we use that baseline to come up with our weekly and daily rates.

For example, take a home with a monthly rental rate of $8,000. We would use the monthly price divided by four and then add 50% to arrive at the weekly rate. ($8,000/4) x 1.5 = $3,000

Once we have the weekly rate, we break down farther to arrive at the daily rate. Using the weekly rate of $3,000 we would divide it by 7 and then add 40% rounding up to get an even number. ($3,000/7) x 1.4 = $586

If we know that weekends are busier rental times than weekdays, we may adjust the weekend rate higher and the weekday rate lower. This is where our expert knowledge of the market is a benefit to you. You can be assured that you are getting the best rental rates.

## Operations

In my opinion, one of the biggest benefits to using a property management company is in having an advocate, acting in your best interest, to handle the business in your absence. All the nitty-gritty details are taken care of – you just sit back, make major decisions only, and enjoy your added income.

First and foremost in the nitty-gritty category, and often the most stressful for an owner, is dealing with renters. Finding them and keeping the good ones that is. Here's where our years of experience really shine. We know the warning signs to look for in prospective renters. Think of us as the moat and drawbridge around your property. We know how to get you high quality tenants and avoid rental scams. Our consistent application and screening process protects you from discrimination lawsuits too.

Once the ideal renter applies, our 24/7 reservation process makes it easy for them to schedule their stay. Whether they call the office or they go online, there is always someone available to help them get booked. When a change needs to be made, we take care of cancellations and re-bookings. We handle all payments and deposits.

We do personalized check-ins for all our guests at our welcome centers located in Scottsdale and at each resort. Here guests receive their package containing keys and directions to the rental property. We also use this opportunity to make a copy of the guest's driver's license for our file. By confirming the renter's identity, we can verify the person checking-in to your home is the same person who made the reservation and that the number of guests in residence is the number of guests they denoted on their application.

In addition, every owner and guest is surveyed electronically upon check-out. All surveys are measured to find trends, problems, and points of excellence in both service and facilities. Owners are notified through the software when there are issues with their property. We then work with you, or on our own, to provide solutions. Our custom-built survey allows us to select which comments will be posted to social media and on our website reviews.

All of our maids and maintenance staff are given iPads loaded with our exclusive software. This enables our team to communicate issues, cleaning status, and take photos of damage and repairs. They can also create work orders in the field and coordinate efficiently with each other. These property management apps are just one example of an industry first that did not exist before we created them.

Using our cutting-edge online technology owner portal you can check the status of your property at any time. You have access to an exclusive smartphone app that integrates directly with our software. This app allows you to see your reservation calendar and make your own reservation. You are also able to create work orders for your property with photos of what you want fixed and update your inventory items by submitting photos of the items, receipts for new items, or removing existing items from the list.

For our Sea Side Reservations clients we have a bill pay service available. Our knowledgeable staff ensures that your bills are paid to the correct Mexican authority for services such as internet, electricity, and insurance. You also have access to the system so you can readily see your balances in both pesos and dollars. You'll never have to waste your precious beach time with these routine activities.

As you can see, one of the things that make us unique from other property managers is the amount of communication we have with our owners. Our software has been customized so that you may set the level of involvement and notification that is right for you. Regardless, the system is available to you 24/7 whenever you want to view your records.

But we don't just "push" information to you. We are also firmly committed to responding when you contact us. Our belief is that all emails should be answered within 24 hours. We monitor and measure our adherence to this standard on a weekly basis and take steps quickly to rectify any issues that keep us from meeting it.

## Property Maintenance

Your property is inspected prior to and immediately following a guest's stay. Although we try to be as thorough as possible, if your property is particularly popular, we may have only a short three hours to "turn" the rental: getting it totally cleaned and restocked for a new tenant. So even with our best efforts we might not always catch a broken plate or a hand towel that went missing. These would be the types of things that fall under wear and tear – a concept we'll cover in more depth in a later chapter.

However, there may be things that our routine inspection might not turn up. These would be things only an occupant would notice. For example, our staff will ensure that if your home is supposed to have a hair-dryer in each bathroom – there really is one in each bathroom. What they won't know is whether or not those hair-dryers actually work. The same might be true for a coffee maker or an iron. We often need feedback from renters or owners regarding these types of issues.

When it comes to repairs, major or minor, we have in-house maintenance staff and/or a network of licensed, bonded and insured contractors. These are providers with whom we have built relationships and know that they provide quality service at a reasonable price. Your renters also have access to 24/7 on-call emergency maintenance so you never have to worry that you'll get a call in the middle of the night.

Safety, security, and protection of your property are primary concerns. So our basic maintenance also extends to at least monthly visits and inspections if, for any reason, your property is not occupied for a period of time. Our goal is to catch minor issues before they become major problems. In many markets we also provide electronic locks that record the time and date of any entry into your home. These locks are state-of-the-art and provide an audit trail that cannot be changed by anyone in our office.

# OWNERSHIP RESPONSIBILTY

While it is our goal to make rental ownership as hassle and stress free as possible, there are still certain areas that fall under the category of owner responsibility. I'm going to go into each of these in detail.

### Homeowners' Association (HOA)

An HOA is an organization that sets rules and regulations for a community. You would have been informed prior to closing whether or not your property is governed by an HOA and you would have received a copy of the Covenants, Conditions and Restrictions (CC&Rs), the Articles of Incorporation, and the Bylaws of this non-profit corporation.

HOAs exist to maintain the value of your property by imposing certain standards for all homeowners and by maintaining any common areas within the development. It is important that you understand the restrictions of your HOA and state, particularly as it relates to rentals. Some HOAs impose minimum times on rentals. For example an owner may be allowed to rent their property monthly, but not weekly. Some HOAs are friendly to allowing vacation rentals but some may charge an "impact" fee to offset what they feel may be excess damage caused by transient renters.

The HOA will likely have architectural requirements such as the colors of outside paint, the types of landscaping, whether or not satellite dishes are allowed, etc. Often there will be approval forms that must be submitted. This type of information is critical for us to know so that we can maintain your property in accordance with the HOA.

Then there are the regulations around uses of your property. For example, a client of mine owned a condo whose HOA restricted them from parking their vehicle in their driveway overnight. Another had strict rules about when you could set your garbage cans out and how soon after trash pick-up you had to have them back in the garage or otherwise out of sight. There may even be restrictions on the number or kind of pets you may keep.

If there are any changes to your HOA CCRs, please notify us immediately. That way we can ensure that the renters are also aware of what they can and cannot do and keep you hassle free. You'd be amazed at how many HOAs have participating owners who like nothing better than to drive around their neighborhoods looking for violations to report.

Generally once a violation has been noted, you will receive a letter asking that it be corrected and/or that a fine has been assessed. The fines might be small depending on the infraction, but if you don't pay them, they become liens against the property which may raise questions in a buyer should you decide to sell. Please give us a call whenever you receive a citation from your HOA.

## **Insurance**

Just as for your primary residence, it is your responsibility to maintain insurance on your rental property. This includes liability insurance as well as property damage insurance. Policies for rentals are commonly called Rental Dwelling Policies, Landlord Policies, or Townhouse/Condo Dwelling Policies and can be obtained through most insurance carriers.

The property damage insurance must be in an amount equal to the replacement cost of the property. Liability insurance must be a minimum of five hundred thousand dollars ($500,000) for each occurrence. Signature Vacation Rentals or Sea Side Reservations should be named as an additional insured. There is generally no cost, or at most a minimal charge, to have us added.

## Home Warranties

While we're on the subject of insurance, let's discuss home warranties. A common misconception is that these are insurance policies. They are not. They're a service contract.

You may have received a Home Warranty from the seller when you bought your home. These are usually good for one year and then the home warranty company will attempt to get you to continue your coverage. While a home warranty may give you peace of mind in your primary residence, we don't recommend them for rental properties, particularly for appliances and air conditioning and here's why:

1. They are not quick to respond to your needs. So for example, let's say you have a unit whose air conditioning goes out in the middle of summer and the warranty company can't get anyone out to even look at it for 3 days; well then you've got some pretty upset renters. Same thing is true if a major appliance like a stove or a washer goes out.

2. Home warranty companies are notoriously difficult to work with. In fact, they lead the list of most complained about companies in America in the 500 categories tracked by Angie's List.

3. You are limited to using their contractors meaning that you have to contact the warranty

company first to find out who services your area, then attempt to make an appointment with them.

4. They don't always cover the entire cost of the repair or replacement. There is often a deductible and always a service call fee. To top it off, the replacement may not be of the same quality that was originally installed.

Needing to deal with a home warranty company to fix a problem when a renter is in your unit seriously ties our hands in how quickly we can make that renter happy. In our opinion, you are better off saving $50 a month and putting it into a rental repair fund than you are spending that $500 or $600 per year for a home warranty.

If you do have a warranty company we will do our best and make every effort to work with them. However, if their response time is such that it will impede the satisfaction of a renter, then it may be necessary for us to respond instead. We would do this in emergency situations but always contact you in advance of doing so.

### Repairs and Maintenance

One of the best things about having a property manager is that we handle all the calls from your renters regarding any problems. Our phones are staffed 24/7. We also take care of routine repairs and maintenance to prevent problems from occurring. Our pre and post inspections are designed specifically for this purpose.

Depending on your contract agreement, there will be a certain dollar limit under which it is in our discretion to make repairs. Over that limit and we will always contact you first to discuss options. For example, if a coffee maker goes out we will replace it without making a call because the cost is low. But if the water heater goes out and needs to be replaced we will not do anything until talking with you. Although in either case, if there is a renter in the unit then time is of the essence. So in emergency situations, if we don't hear from you quickly we will move forward with providing a solution.

Some owners prefer to contract with their own vendors for routine maintenance like landscaping or pool service. But we highly recommend that you allow us to use ours. When you have a guest in your rental and something goes wrong, you need to get it repaired quickly and with minimum interruption to the guest. That is the level of service they expect for the money they have paid.

Our relationship with our vendors is such that we can demand this type of service. Your provider may not be quite so responsive. Let's say for example that your pool is cleaned on Wednesday. A new guest moves into the rental on Friday. On Saturday a major storm whips through the area throwing debris into the pool. Your guest expects the pool to be cleaned but your service provider is more likely to say that they won't be out until the following Wednesday because you've contracted for weekly service.

The service providers we use have been thoroughly vetted for quality. In addition, because we have them working on multiple properties, we are often in a better position to negotiate preferred pricing which can save you money in the long run.

## **Wear and Tear versus Damages**

As I mentioned in the introduction to this book, making the distinction between what constitutes normal wear and tear versus damages is the area over which there is much confusion. I am hoping that by providing some examples of each in the paragraphs below it will help us avoid most issues.

Wear and tear is defined as the damage that naturally and inevitably occurs as a result of normal aging and use. It is the depreciation of an asset that is assumed to occur even when an item is used competently and with care and proper maintenance. Even the most conscientious tenant will cause minor damage over the course of a rental agreement, particularly if it is long-term. Wear and tear is unavoidable and there is a certain amount that you as an owner should expect every year. Damages on the other hand are things that are out of the ordinary.

Linens are a great example of items that routinely experience wear and tear. An independent survey of several linen suppliers calculated the average linen replacement factors listed below for vacation rental owners. "Uses" is another way of saying the number of reservations.

Flat Sheet – 58.6 uses
Fitted Sheet – 42.4 uses
Pillow Case – 21.3 uses
Bath Towel – 18.2 uses
Face Towel – 11.4 uses
Washcloth – 4 uses
Bath Mat – 22.3 uses
Kitchen Linens – 1.76 uses

Here are some other examples of the difference between wear and tear that you should expect, and damages that would be charged to the guest.

Dirty carpet in main traffic areas or small, light stains would be considered wear and tear. Burn marks, rips, pet urine, or heavy stains like red wine are damages.

Scuff marks or small nicks on walls are wear and tear. Deep gouges, holes, torn wallpaper, crayon marks, and scratches or chew marks from pets constitute damages.

Blind pulls or strings may be worn or frayed due to constant use. The internal strings that pull the blinds up and down may also become damaged from sun exposure and break – all normal wear and tear. Blinds or curtains that are torn, stained, or pulled from the frame are signs of damage.

Other things that could be construed as damages would be: a yard dug up by a pet, excessive mildew in a bathroom caused by an unreported leak, excessive dirt in other parts of the home that requires professional cleaning to remove, drains that are clogged from inserting foreign objects or items that should not be put in a drain, wood floors with deep scratches, or broken tiles on a relatively new floor that are not the result of poor installation.

Those that would be normal wear and tear would be: replacement of component parts like faucet washers, water heater elements, or pool filters. Also, if a single plate or glass is broken, or a spoon is missing, or there's a small blood stain on a towel – it is wear and tear. If several plates are broken, several pieces of silver missing, or several towels bloodstained or missing from the same renter – it would be damages.

The bottom line is that the difference between wear and tear and damages is often a judgement call. In all cases, we strive to be fair and ethical to both you and your guest. That being said, as an owner you should plan for and set aside money for those items that are normal wear and tear.

## Safety and Security

It is your responsibility as a rental property owner to ensure as much as possible the safety and security of your guests.

Here are some tips for how to keep your guests safe and secure:

1. Make sure any heavy appliances are secured. For example, if you have a large screen TV on a console it should be secured so that a small child cannot easily tip it over.

2. In pool areas, ensure that filters are properly covered to prevent someone's hair or clothing from being sucked in. Have access to the pool secured from young children to prevent drowning. Install non-slip texturing around the pool area if possible.

3. Provide ample outdoor lighting. Use motion activated lighting if you have a single-family rental and ensure that lighting on the walkway to and from the doors is good.

4. The fire extinguisher system should be in good working order and smoke detectors should be installed to warn guests if a fire occurs.

5. Trim back bushes and trees from windows and doors on the property. This eliminates places for burglars to hide. In states like Arizona and California, it also helps to keep wildfires from spreading to the residence.

6. Install durable doors with deadbolts.

7. Make sure your sliding glass doors and windows have anti-theft mechanisms. For example, use a through-the-frame pin for windows that open vertically or a dowel that fits in the track for windows that open horizontally. The dowel approach can also be used to secure a sliding glass door, or a security bar can be installed. The idea is to make a break-in less likely.

8. Consider installing a monitored alarm system even if your state or city doesn't require it.

Breakdowns in any security measures that you have in place should be considered an emergency and fixed immediately. You want to do everything you can to limit your liability and protect your guests, just as you would in your own home.

## Taxes

First let me begin by saying I am not an accountant nor am I a tax specialist. This section is simply intended to make you aware of some of the taxes that may impact your ownership of a vacation rental. I strongly urge you to consult your own accountant or tax specialist for professional assistance.

There are basically three types of taxes that may affect you and your rental property: income tax, compliance taxes, and property tax.

**Income tax:** Any income that you generate from the rental of your property must be reported as income tax. We will provide you with a 1099-MISC statement for the gross amount of your rentals for the year. You may be able to deduct certain expenses related to the rental depending on how often it was occupied and how often you used the home. Check with your accountant to determine what might apply as each situation is different. A complete Profit and Loss statement is available to you through the Owner Portal that summarizes all income and expenses for the year.

**Compliance tax:** This tax may also be known as sales tax, occupancy tax, lodging tax, transient tax, room tax, or hotel tax. They are paid on the total amount of the rental fee. Depending on where your property is located the tax may also be charged on things like cleaning services, maintenance fees, or pet fees. Basically anything that you charge the renter is subject to the tax. These taxes are payable to the state, city or county depending on your location. They are often confusing as different rates and payment dates (monthly or quarterly) may apply.

Fortunately, we make this part of paying taxes hassle free for the owners in our program. We collect the taxes from the renters, file the tax returns, and remit payments on your behalf. All you need to do is acquire your tax license and provide us with that information.

**Property tax:** This is the tax assessed by the state, county and/or city where your rental property is located. If you took out a loan for the property then it's likely that your property tax is part of an escrow payment that your bank then remits on a semi-annual basis. If not, then your property tax statement will come directly to you. It is your responsibility to ensure that this tax is paid.

# SETTING GUEST EXPECTATIONS

When a potential guest is researching a rental property for their vacation they are generally looking at three things: location, internal and external amenities, and price. I talked earlier about pricing and how it is affected by location and seasonality. Since you've already purchased your vacation rental, those two items have been pre-determined. What hasn't is what you put in and around your home. This also has a major impact on the price you can charge and fortunately, it is one you can control.

External amenities are those things that surround your home, for example: a pool, a spa, a barbeque pit, or a casita. Heated pools in particular can significantly affect the price and rental occupancy in "snowbird" markets.

It may also include your proximity to restaurants, shopping, events, and medical care. The amenities offered in or near the property add to the potential enjoyment of your guests. The more of these you have, and the higher the quality, the more you can charge for your property.

Equally important, but often overlooked are the amenities inside your home. These include not only the layout and design of your home, i.e. number of bedrooms, number of bathrooms, etc. but also the home's furnishings and inventory. Let's take a look at each of these in more detail.

## Internal Amenities

By far the most important internal amenity is the one listed above – number of bedrooms. But it isn't just the number that is important. It's also the size and comfort of the bed, easy access to a bathroom, and suitable closet space.

En-suite bathrooms are the most desirable and can garner a higher rental value. Especially if they are equipped with Jacuzzi tubs, multi-head shower systems, dual sinks, or heated floors. And don't forget the lighting – ample lighting in the bath-room is a must for make-up application. The lack of it can give a bad start to your female guest's day.

Other examples of internal amenities would be a separate laundry room, workout room, three-car garage, or an in-home theater.

Wireless internet access and cable, or satellite TV, are no longer "nice to haves." In today's online world, your property must come with these in order to compete. Internet speed should be fast – no one wants to wait 30 seconds or more for a website to load. I also recommend your television service provide at least one premium channel.

## **Furnishings**

Furnishings are things like appliances, couches, chairs, tables, beds, and permanent fixtures such as built-ins and lighting in the home. You are listing your property as a "luxury" vacation rental and as such, a guest will have certain expectations regarding the quality of the furnishings they will find upon arrival. Studies have shown that the first 9 minutes of a stay will lock in 80% of a guest's opinion of their entire experience in your rental.

In all cases you should strive for the highest quality you can afford but you also need to insure its durability. While a gray satin couch might look stunning in the family room, it stains easily and is difficult to clean. The same could be said for a white shag rug. It may look trendy and rich but in a high traffic area its deep piles will collect dirt and without frequent cleaning it may soon become an eyesore.

Another thing to keep in mind when choosing furnishings for your vacation rental is decorating trends. The interior design industry estimates that homeowners redecorate every five years to keep their homes looking fresh. This can get quite expensive when you're talking about changing out couches or carpet. But your guests are expecting a fresh and modern vacation rental, not one that is dated.

So what do you do? Start with neutrals in all your major pieces. For kitchen appliances that means going with stainless steel. Stainless steel has been a mainstay in kitchens for the last century and no one predicts its obsolescence anytime soon. It adds a polished finish to any décor and seamlessly matches with all color schemes.

Couches, love seats, tables and chairs should match the "vibe" of wherever your vacation rental is located. So for example, if your property is located near the beach, you may have wicker furniture. If you are in the mountains, a more rustic wood finish would be appropriate, and in the desert you might go with a southwest flare. What you don't want to do is put ultra-modern, minimalist, sterile pieces in a cozy, mountain chalet or wicker-based furniture in a New York City high-rise.

Regardless of location you'll want your fabrics in neutral colors like gray, tan, taupe, black, and sand. I would warn against pure white unless it is in a highly wearable, easy to clean fabric. When choosing fabric also keep in mind how it will be used. If your rental is a beach property you should expect that oils and lotions will get on the furniture. You'll need a fabric that repels oils or at least cleans well.

Location will determine what other special amenities you might need to have. For example, if you have a ski chalet you'll need to make sure that there is a place for renters to leave their boots and snow-covered clothes where they won't harm your floors or furniture. In a beach location you'll want to stay away from rugs that will collect sand no matter how often you vacuum.

I also recommend that when you are thinking about window treatments you choose those that are uncomplicated and least likely to break. For that reason I like to see rod and ring type curtains rather than string pull curtains or shades. Everyone knows how to open them, the rings rarely break and the curtains are easy to take down, clean and replace.

Window treatments should also block a great deal of light when pulled. A common complaint that we receive from guests is that the shades, blinds or curtains do not block enough of the sunlight. I recently stayed at the hotel in San Jose Del Cabo and I really appreciated that the window had enough blocking ability to keep the room dark during the day. It was an east facing room and I had travelled all night to get there. Having a dark room made it easier for me to rejuvenate.

The style of your bedroom furniture should also match the motif of your location. A king size bed is a must in the master bedroom if space permits. We've had renters pass on the ideal place simply because the master bedroom had a queen instead of a king. Guest bedrooms may contain queen size beds or two twin beds.

When deciding what to do with your guest room, take into account your target market for renters. If you're going after male golfers or families with older children, then twin beds might make sense. If the majority of your renters will be couples or parents with younger children then queens or kings are the way to go. You may also want to scope out the competition before deciding. If everyone has queens in the second bedroom then you may want to set yourself apart by having twins. Be sure to contact us if you'd like help with making this decision.

Mattresses should be medium-firm and, unless the bed is a platform model, they should be set on a box-spring. Memory foam is also great for accommodating the majority of sleepers' needs. Cushion top mattress pads are recommended for added comfort. Just make sure that you get ones that won't trap heat. Renters will pull them off if they make the bed uncomfortable.

Other items that should be in each bedroom include a newer model television and clock radio with an alarm. Reading lamps on each side of the bed are also necessary.

Once you have the basic furnishings it is easy to keep your property looking fresh. A new coat of paint in a trending color, plus accent pieces like throw pillows, vases, and wall art that can be swapped out at minimal expense are all it takes.

You may want to consider utilizing the expertise of an interior designer when determining how to decorate and furnish your rental. A designer often has a better feel for what works in the area, can steer you in the right direction in terms of color usage, and has access to deals with suppliers that could save you a significant amount of money. A beautifully decorated property that meets guest expectations helps to keep them coming back again and again.

**Inventory**

Inventory may be thought of as all the wear and tear types of items you typically would find in a home. This would include kitchen and bathroom linens, small appliances like coffee makers and vacuums, pots and pans, dinnerware, silverware, garbage cans, irons and ironing boards, etc. A full list of the items that should be in each rental unit can be found in Appendix A. You may have already received this list or a similar one in your welcome packet.

As with furnishings, you should equip your unit with the highest quality of inventory items that you can afford. Fortunately today there are several stores that sell luxury items at a discounted price: Kohl's, Target, HomeGoods, Marshalls, Gordman's and Living Spaces to name a few. However, if you are deep in Mexico you may need to get your items from local sources.

Nowhere is quality more of an issue than in the bedroom. For many people, the bedroom is their oasis. Bedding must be inviting, stylish and scream luxury. If the current bedding trend is to have multiple decorative pillows, then you need to have multiple decorative pillows. Coverlets may look great alone but if you really want to impress you need a coverlet and a high-end comforter.

In a market where you are required to provide sheets, they should be luxurious as well. A thread count of 400 or more is recommended. Sateen sheets work well – they wash the best and look nice. Avoid microfiber. Though white sheets may not last as long as colored sheets, they still are the number one look: symbolizing elegant simplicity.

White is the color that guests used to staying in high-end hotels have come to expect. Hotels spend fortunes funding studies to understand guest psychology. The results show a primal association between the color white and cleanliness. If you see crisp white sheets you instantly know they are clean. Sheets that are some other color like gray or maroon might be clean but who knows? Those colors hide dirt and guests subconsciously know this. Bright freshly laundered sheets look clean and therefore appear more sanitary.

White sheets are easier to clean and maintain which may sound counter-intuitive. However, they can be bleached and washed in hot water which keeps them whiter, longer. Plus they always match. White is white. You don't have to buy a full set if all you need to replace are some pillow cases.

If you need to provide the bathroom linens, be aware that they are next on the list in terms of quality. Bath towels should be plush and hold up well when washed. No one likes to dry themselves off with something that feels like sandpaper. Believe me I've been in many a luxury hotel where the towels felt just like that. It wasn't a pleasant experience and made me wonder why I was paying top dollar to stay there.

It's also important to have matching white linens and towels throughout the home. It gives your home a "put together" feel. It also makes it easier for the staff to ready your home again once the laundry has been done.

Quality may be less distinguishable in the balance of the other items of inventory in your home. For example, there isn't a noticeable difference in performance between a silverware set that costs $70 and one that costs $150, or a kitchen towel that costs $6 versus one that costs $9. Given the fact that these items need to be replaced frequently, it may even be advisable to go the less expensive route.

What is important for silverware, dinnerware, or pots and pans is that you consider how easy it will be to match the current set with replacement pieces in the future. Simple white plates with rounded shapes are much easier to replace than a seasonal design. It's helpful to us if you take a picture of the box that your items came in so we know exactly the style and the manufacturer.

When buying look for items that say "open stock." These are the easiest to replace although sometimes it's possible for us to find out of date lines on eBay or Amazon. You started with matching sets of flatware, dishes, pots, pans and storage containers and you want to maintain that appearance. Your kitchen drawers and cabinets should never look like everything came from a garage sale.

Closets, drawers, and cabinets regardless of where they are in your home should be free of any of your personal effects. Find an area in your home, perhaps a laundry room closet or storage area in the garage, that can be locked and store your personal items there. That way they are secure and not accessible to renters or staff.

The bottom line is to put yourself in the shoes of the guest who is renting your property. What quality would you expect for the price you are expecting your guests to pay? If you must budget, do it somewhere other than the bedrooms or bathrooms.

## Inspections Before and After

I touched on these inspections when speaking about the benefits of having a property management company service your rental. Inspections are good for you the owner ensuring that the guest pays for any damages sustained while renting and they are good for the guest as well ensuring that they are not charged for damages that existed prior to their rental.

We perform a full inspection when we first take your property under management. This includes taking photos of each room so we have a visual record of the condition and the furnishings. These photos are also used to market your property. In addition we take photos of all of your inventory items. We do ask you to provide a complete listing of everything that is in your rental and to update the list annually.

As a reminder, our 21-point monthly maintenance inspection includes:

- Monthly physical presence at the house in between tenants

-   Replacing of standard light bulbs, air filters, and batteries
-   Removal of flyers and mailers from doors and driveway
-   Flushing all toilets and checking for leaks
-   Verification that landscaping and pool services are on schedule
-   Visual inspection of the outside of the property
-   Check-out maintenance inspection after guest departure

Ongoing inspections of the property are particularly important when the rental is not occupied. Often guests will inform us of problems or issues in the survey that we ask them to complete at the end of their stay. When the unit has been unoccupied for a period of time we rely on our monthly visits to ensure that we catch any minor issues before they become major problems.

If you are fortunate enough to have tenants the majority of the time, we may not always be able to do a full count of every inventory item in the check-out maintenance inspection. Sometimes the turnaround time between one guest checking out and the next checking in is too tight to allow for this. That is great news for you in terms of rental income!

Guests will generally call us if anything isn't working properly, something is missing, or there isn't enough of an item. Rest assured we will do a full inventory as often as time allows. It is in our best interest, and yours, to keep the unit in great condition and fully stocked.

## To Pet or Not To Pet

That is indeed the question and it comes up frequently. I usually advise against allowing pets in your rental. However, times they are a changin' as Bob Dylan would say.

The American Pet Products Association estimates that Americans own 83 million dogs and 95 million cats. That means 50% of "homeowners" have at least one dog and 45% have a least one cat. That's a pretty large segment of the population. And pet owners love their pets – sometimes I think more than they love their own children!

Pet owners tend to have higher incomes and they are more likely to want to vacation with their pets, particularly if they are going to be gone for an extended period of time. More and more high-end, boutique hotels are becoming "pet friendly" for this very reason.

Even given this trend I still lean toward no pets. However, here are some of the pros and cons to pet or not to pet so that you can make an informed decision.

## Pros:

1. A larger pool of potential guests to draw from. In addition those guests tend to rent for longer periods of time.

2. Your property may become more desirable because there aren't as many options to choose from.

3. You can charge a higher rent and increase your revenue stream.

4. A guest who really can't be without their dog or cat may bring them anyway. Even though you and we, have specifically said that pets are not allowed. Even though they have checked the box on the rental agreement that states they won't be bringing any pets into the unit.

## Cons:

1. Potential for damage to the property. You should consider the cost to replace or repair the furnishings and surroundings of your rental. Large dogs can mar hardwood floors. All dogs, particularly females, can turn the grass brown from urination. And if any pet, dog or cat, urinates in the house itself carpet may need to be replaced. Dogs may gnaw on cabinets or door jambs and cats may scratch those and furniture as well. Will the potential cost of replacement or the lack of usability while repairs are being made outweigh the increased rental?

2. Physical injury to neighbors or other guests that your renter invites into the home. A dog bite or cat scratch can be quite serious.

3. Pets may cause a noise nuisance particularly if the guest is off doing fun things for the majority of the day and the pet is left alone. Both cats and dogs have been known to meow or bark until their owners return.

4. Allergens and dander will find their way deep into your carpets and into the air ducts. Even with a very thorough cleaning it is difficult to eliminate these entirely. This may cause problems for future guests who have pet allergies.

While the following are not pros or cons they are things you should take into consideration as well when making your decision.

1. What type of rental unit do you have? Check with your Condo Association or HOA to determine their restrictions on pets. Also keep in mind that a condo with walls that are shared by connected neighbors may be prone to noise complaints. Do you want to have to deal with letters from your Association and possible fines? The irony is that most Condo Associations have a limit on the weight of the pet, usually 50 lbs. or less. These small pets are often the most excitable and "yappy."

2. Does your insurance policy cover damage from pets that are not yours? And even more important, does your liability coverage protect you from paying for physical injury caused to another by a guest's pet?

3. If you do decide that the benefits of allowing pets outweigh the risks, consider having your attorney draft a pet agreement as an addendum to the standard rental agreement that everyone would sign, regardless of whether or not they were bringing a pet. In the agreement you might include things like: how many pets are allowed (limit to 2), the size of the pets (50lbs or less), who pays for additional cleaning or damage if needed, requiring papers showing pets have been spayed or neutered and have all their vaccinations.

4. Check the Americans with Disabilities Act (ADA) and Fair Housing Association (FHA) rules, both State and Federal, for the area in which your rental property resides. If a guest, or you as a rental property owner, fall under these parameters the guest may be allowed to bring a Service, Guide, Signal, or Support animal with them regardless of whether or not you typically allow pets. One exception is if allowing the pet would cause "undue hardship" on the property owner. An example of undue hardship would be if you had a severe allergic reaction to pet dander. In that case you may be able refuse to accept pets under the ADA.

## Boats, Trucks, and Vacation Rentals

You're probably wondering why, in a book about owning a vacation rental, I've decided to talk about boats and trucks. Well it's quite simple really – they're all things your friends and family like to use.

Ever notice when you get a new boat how everyone is suddenly interested in going to the lake? Or when you get a new truck how family, friends, or friends of friends suddenly have all kinds of things they need moved or picked up? And hey, they'd be happy to pay for gas, or get you a pizza and a six pack. You've instantly become the most popular person in town.

The same will be true as soon as word gets out that you now own a vacation rental. And the sweeter the location the more bees you will attract. Now I'm not saying that you shouldn't ever share the bounty with your family and friends but I would caution you to be smart about it.

You originally decided to rent your vacation home because: a) you want to offset the cost of your mortgage and upkeep and/or b) you want to make additional income. Renting to family and friends rarely does either of those, particularly if you are renting during "the season" when you could have been bringing in top dollar. Just as we recommend that you not use your property during season, we also strongly encourage you to not rent at a discount to friends and family as well.

But we also know it's hard to say no, especially to family. That's why we're here. We can let you off the hook in terms of being the bad guy. All you have to do is let them know that you have a contract with a property management company and that they need to contact us about rental arrangements and payment. Problem solved.

If you do decide to rent your unit to friends, please don't block out the time as if it were for you. If you want to charge them a discounted fee, that's fine. Let us know and have them book the rental through us. We perform the same amount of high quality work regardless of who is in the unit to earn our commission. We've made a commitment to treat you ethically and fairly. Please give us the same consideration.

*"A vacation spot out of season always has a very special magic."* Max von Sydow, actor

# SUMMARY

Once again I'd like to say thank you for joining the Signature Vacation Rentals and Sea Side Reservation family. I hope that you will find this guidebook a handy resource to refer to time and again as you settle into your role as a vacation rental property owner.

Remember we have made it our number one priority to meet the needs of our homeowners. Our mission is to provide an unmatched guest and owner experience with 100% satisfaction. You may contact us at:

Toll free U.S. 877.976.1234

Toll free Canada 800.527.4059

info@arizonalodgingexperts.com

SignatureVacationRentals.com

# ABOUT THE AUTHOR

Steve Schwab is the Founder and Chief Executive Officer of the Schwab Organization, the parent company of Signature Vacation Rentals and Sea Side Vacation Rentals. He has been in the vacation rental business since graduating from New Mexico State University – over 15 years.

As a former member of the U.S. Army Special Operations community, Steve has a unique understanding of what it takes to establish delivery systems that are goal focused. For the vacation rental property management industry this means putting the right people and processes in place to ensure that all of an owner's needs are met in a timely, transparent, and exceptional manner.

Steve is a pioneer in performance driven industry software. His position as managing partner in Streamline Vacation Rental Software has allowed him to create many industry "first" technologies that continue to change the market. His creative work has been featured in numerous publications and television appearances.

But his commitment to excellence doesn't stop with technology. It is a value that is instilled in everyone who works with and for the organization. Steve's emphasis on ethics and world class performance has been exemplified in exclusive resorts and estates in ten cities and two countries.

Steve is always looking for others who share his values and interest in providing stellar property management. If this is you, franchise opportunities do exist.

You may contact Steve at:
steve@signaturevacationrentals.com

# OUR COMPANY

Signature Vacation Rentals and Sea Side Reservations are part of the Schwab Organization family of companies.

Founded in 2000, Sea Side Reservations began business as Cyndi's Beach House Rentals – a struggling company that Steve purchased from its owner and then rapidly grew into the largest vacation rental company in Mexico. Its offices are located in Puerto Peñasco, San Carlos, Ensenada, Puerto Vallarta, Cancun, and Playa del Carmen.

Signature Vacation Rentals began operation in 2008 in Scottsdale, Arizona. Originally begun as a way to take advantage of seasonality in the market – Mexico's season is May to August while Arizona's season is October to February – it also quickly grew to become one of the premier luxury vacation rental property management firms.

The success of our companies is due in large part to Steve's leadership and his laser focus on the owner, the renter, and exemplary service for both. Paying attention to detail promptly and professionally is our requisite standard, not a lofty or seldom attainable ideal. We are dedicated to establishing and retaining the clientele for whom we provide exceptional management services. Our objective is to be the best at what we do.

To that end, we have Sea Side University and the ORANGE program for bringing our vision and culture to all employees, whether in Mexico or the U.S.

Sea Side University is our own private educational institution. Its mission is to train and educate employees in our company so that everyone knows exactly what is expected. Basic training is provided to all workers, including but not limited to: Reservations, the Front Desk, Maid Service, Maintenance and Security.

After finishing the basic training, a new employee will be able to start working in his/her area at 100% competence and efficiency. They will also have been cross-trained to help out in other areas of the company. In addition to the basic training, we offer courses to strengthen and improve the skills of our team members and hold regular refresher courses. This is a program that few, if any, other property management firms employ.

But we don't stop there. We recognize, particularly in the Mexican market, that there can be major cultural and language differences between our employees, our owners and our renters. The ORANGE program was started to ensure that the gap in these differences could be closed in a manner consistent throughout the company. ORANGE is a visual and conversational way of imparting our vision and mission to everyone. It is re-enforced through regularly scheduled meetings where each of its tenets are discussed using real-world examples.

O – Owner Centric

> Our philosophy is the Owners are at the Center of all we do. They are the reason we have a business and our company is dedicated to ensuring their happiness and success.

R – Renters

> Our goal must be to convert Renters into Raving fans. If they have checked out and have not been impressed then we have failed them and we have failed ourselves.

A – Anticipate

> Our purpose is to anticipate the unexpressed wants and needs of the Customer.

N – Never lose . . .

> Never lose an Owner or Guest's confidence in our ability to deliver excellence. Instant guest pacification is the responsibility of each

employee. Whoever receives a complaint will own it, resolve it to the guest's satisfaction and record it.

G – Go the Extra Mile

Every day with every customer and coworker, you are the ambassador for Sea Side Reservations and Signature Vacation Rentals. You must perform above and beyond every time you have an interaction with anyone inside or outside the company.

E – Excellence

Our vision can only be achieved by delivering excellence in everything we do. If you see anything that is happening that is not performed with excellence then it is your responsibility to fix it and help improve it so that it doesn't happen again.

We believe that this program is also unique to the market, particularly with our focus on YOU – the owner.

# APPENDIX A
Minimum Recommended Furnishings
and Accessories

<u>Kitchen</u>

Baking Dish
Blender
Cake Pan
Can Opener
Cheese Grater
Coffee Mugs
Coffee Maker (Auto Shut Off)
Colander
Cookie Sheets
Cooking Tools – Ladle, Spatula, Spoon, etc.
Cookware Set – Stainless Steel Preferred –
Circulon
Corkscrew Cutting Board (2)
Dinnerware – Designer Line
   1 BR – Service for 4
   2 BR – Service for 8
   3 BR – Service for 12
   4 BR – Service for 16
   5 BR – Service for 18

Fire Extinguisher

Flatware – Best Quality
>    1 BR – Service for 4
>    2 BR – Service for 8
>    3 BR – Service for 12
>    4 BR – Service for 16
>    5 BR – Service for 18

Food Storage Containers – Bowls & Lids

Glassware
>    1 BR – Service for 4
>    2 BR – Service for 8 including:
>        Stemmed Glasses
>        Drinking Glasses
>        Beverage / Rocks
>        Plastic cups for pool area

Ice Cream Scoop
Kitchen Knife Set/Block or assorted
Measuring Cups & Spoons
Microwave Oven
Mixing Bowls
Serving Platters and Bowls
Steak Knife Set
Tea Kettle
Toaster / Toaster Oven
Wastebasket
Labeled Recycle Basket if applicable
Decorative pieces
Salt & Pepper Shaker/Grinder
10 to 14-Piece cookware set (pots and pans)
Upgrades: Wok, Pizza stone/pan, pasta boiler,
water filter & other miscellaneous gourmet kitchen

supplies would be listed as Gourmet Kitchen on our web page.

Linens

2 sets of linens for each bed, 200-300 plus count
1 blanket, comforter & bead skirt for each bed
Shams for each pillow
Extra Pillows
2 Towel sets for each prospective guest
1 pool towel for each prospective guest
4+ Dish Cloths and Dish Towels
2+ Pot Holders
Placemat & Cloth Napkin for each dining table seat

Bathrooms

Bath Set for each bathroom including:
> Bath Rugs
> Shower Curtain
> Soap Dish
> Toothbrush Holder
> Toilet Brush and Holder

Waste Basket
Hair Dryer

Miscellaneous

Voice Mail or Answering Machine
Alarm Clock

BBQ & Utensils; Minimum 4 burner Gas Grill
Broom & Dust Pan
Cleaning Supplies: Mop, dust rags, polish, cleaners, etc.
Coasters
Extra Ice Trays
Flashlight
Garden Hose, Hanger and spray nozzle
Clothes Hangers (Platinum Homes should have wooden not plastic hangers)
Iron (Auto Shut Off) & Full Size Ironing Board
Laundry Baskets
Spare Light Bulbs
Mop
Paper Towel Holder
Patio Furniture and Loungers (Avoid Patio Tables with Glass tops)
Plunger
Reading Lamps
Stereo with CD + iPod/MP3 Player Connection
2+ Telephones – 1 Cordless
Flat Screen Televisions: 40" or larger for main living area and recommend 22" or larger TV's for each bedroom.
DVD/BluRay – Minimum 1 for main TV & one for Master Suite
Hi-Speed Internet Connection (Wired/Wireless)
Homes with pools should have a Skimmer and a Brush
Smoke Detectors
10 Piece Tool Set
Garage Ladder (Tall enough to reach the highest light bulb/smoke detector in your house)
Ice Chest/Cooler

*This Signature Vacation Rentals recommended furnishings list is the minimum we think the home should have. Anything over that minimum will be listed and noted as an upgrade on your property page.*

Made in the USA
Lexington, KY
28 October 2016